Original title:
Shadows of the Cedar Song

Copyright © 2025 Creative Arts Management OÜ
All rights reserved.

Author: Micah Sterling
ISBN HARDBACK: 978-1-80567-387-3
ISBN PAPERBACK: 978-1-80567-686-7

Reflections in the Timbered Realm

In the trees, a squirrel prances,
Chasing dreams of nutty glances.
Breezes tickle, leaves go wild,
Nature's laughter, bright and styled.

Under branches, whispers tease,
Jokes exchanged among the bees.
With every crack of twigs around,
The forest sings a joyful sound.

Hues of the Dappled Path

Frogs in chorus, croaking tunes,
Mice in tuxedos dance by moons.
Colorful blooms shake in delight,
Wobbling ants keep the beat right.

Wandering foxes share a joke,
While shy owls ponder, smoke rings choke.
Every step, a funny twist,
In the path where smiles persist.

Harmonics of the Woodland Spirits

Beneath the canopy's embrace,
A band of critters finds its place.
Badgers strumming on leafy strings,
A melody that nature sings.

Raccoons throw a funky ball,
Playful spirits, standing tall.
Giggles echo through the trees,
Laughter drifting with the breeze.

The Dance of Flickering Lights

Fireflies twinkle, quite the sight,
Dancing partner, ghostly night.
With every sway, a story told,
Of silly pranks and mischief bold.

Underneath the starry dome,
Creatures gather, far from home.
With laughter ringing, night takes flight,
Joyful chaos, pure delight.

Vignettes of the Cedar's Breath

In the forest where giggles grow,
Cedar trees sway with a breezy flow.
Squirrels dance, wearing tiny caps,
While rabbits play on their leafy laps.

A fox in boots struts with great flair,
Making all the woodland critters stare.
The owls hoot jokes 'til the sun's eye yawns,
As the raccoons tap dance on the dawn's lawns.

The ants parade with tiny drums,
As shadows play with a wink and hum.
A porcupine croons a silly song,
And all the beetles hum along.

In this glade where laughter rains,
Each breeze carries friendly refrains.
Join the revelry, don't be shy—
For every giggle can make trees sigh.

Dreamscapes in the Woodland Veil

In a realm where giggles bloom,
Beneath the cedar's perfumed gloom.
A mouse with glasses reads a tale,
While toads leap high without a fail.

A dancing leaf caught in mid-flight,
Twirls with a squirrel in delight.
Bunnies in boots hop to the beat,
While a hedgehog plays on loop with his feet.

Chasing shadows that tickle the ground,
Laughter echoes all around.
The fireflies wink with a cheeky grin,
As the moon slips on a sly, silver skin.

Woodland whimsies fill the air,
With every rustle, tales to share.
The night grows bright with tales so tall—
In this woodland hive, there's fun for all.

Through the Folds of Dusk's Cloak

In the dusky twilight, I sway,
With my broomstick horse at play.
The owls hoot a quirky tune,
As I dance with the light of the moon.

Squirrels gossip in the trees,
About the bread crumbs and some cheese.
Beneath the stars that wink and gleam,
I trip and tumble, what a dream!

The shadows stretch, they tickle my toes,
With every giggle, the mischief grows.
A raccoon joins in with a fancy hat,
A juggling act with a flying cat!

In this funny dusk parade we partake,
Skirting puddles that we make.
Each chuckle bounces off the bark,
We're the night's merry, giggling lark!

Reverie in the Grove

In the grove where lilies sigh,
The squirrels dance, oh my, oh my!
A hedgehog sings with great delight,
While shadows prance, avoiding the light.

The flowers snicker, what a sight,
As bees buzz loudly, just a fright.
A rabbit juggles carrots, you see,
While crickets chirp in harmony.

Leaves whisper secrets, they tease and play,
Thinking of silly games all day.
A frog in spectacles croaks a beat,
As nature's ball keeps the fun upbeat!

In this spot, where laughter's made,
We splash in puddles, unafraid.
A merry band of woodland laughing,
Through the night, no sign of quaffing!

Skies that Paint the Ground

The clouds roll in like fluffy sheep,
Painting dreams, oh what a leap!
With colors splashed on fields and trees,
Even the daisies laugh with ease.

A rainbow spills, it skips and hops,
While giggling raindrops plop and plop.
A dog in boots does a funny jig,
As children hop, the dance so big!

The sun winks down with a golden grin,
As squirrels engage in a cheeky spin.
Underneath the painted sky,
Giggling at clouds passing by.

Here, where laughter and colors blend,
Every moment, a new trend.
In this vibrant, playful town,
The ground may shake, but no one frowns!

Fables Woven in the Wind

The breeze tells tales of mischief fair,
With gusty giggles swirling in the air.
A tale of socks lost in the trees,
And sprightly whispers that tease and please.

Branches sway as stories unfold,
Of joyful luau set in gold.
The raccoons mime a circus train,
While otters splash without refrain.

Leaves tickle my nose, giggle in flight,
As the sun fades into the night.
With tales of kites and hats that fly,
The winds weave tales as they pass by.

In this realm of playful jest,
Where every creature is dressed and blessed.
We frolic and laugh till stars arise,
With fables woven beneath the skies!

Whispers Beneath the Canopy

In the forest where giggles reside,
Squirrels gossip, their chattering wide.
Who stole my acorn, they dance with cheer,
While the wise old owl just hoots from near.

Leaves rustle softly, a comedic prank,
As rabbits leap over the bubbling tank.
The mushrooms giggle, in their own little way,
Under moonlight they wiggle and sway.

Echoes of Twilight's Embrace

Bats swoop low with a screechy delight,
While fireflies twinkle, a magical sight.
A raccoon, all clumsy, spills his night snack,
As the trees snicker, they've got his back.

The crickets conspire, with chirps and with grins,
Planning a party to welcome the winds.
Hippos in pajamas join in on the fun,
As laughter abounds under the setting sun.

The Lullaby of Ancient Boughs

The branches croon softly, a tune of delight,
While foxes are twirling, joyous in flight.
With a hop and a skip, they join in the song,
Under the boughs where the giggles belong.

A hedgehog in glasses reads poetry sweet,
While badgers play cards, tapping their feet.
The old trees chuckle, their stories unfold,
As the night wraps around, all whimsical and bold.

Dance of the Silent Pines

Pine trees sway in a rhythmic embrace,
As rabbits and hedgehogs have a wild race.
With each little twirl, a story is spun,
Of dances and mischief and riddles to stun.

The gnomes plot a prank with a wink and a grin,
As mushrooms decide it's time to begin.
The forest erupts in a jubilant cheer,
With laughter and music, the woodland is clear.

Echoing Through the Pine's Embrace

In pines that sway with glee,
A squirrel dances, wild and free.
He trips on branches, oh what a sight,
Leaving behind a trail of delight.

He challenges the wind to a race,
With nuts strewn all over the place.
The birds all chuckle, perched up high,
As he tumbles down with a comical sigh.

The Spirit's Caress in the Boughs

The breeze whispers jokes to the trees,
While leaves crackle, giggling with ease.
A raccoon winks, thinking he's sly,
As he steals a snack, oh me, oh my!

Each branch holds secrets, tales old and new,
Of critters plotting their clever debut.
The forest erupts in laughter and cheer,
As the moon peeks out, lending an ear.

Serenades of the Nightingale's Perch

At dusk, the nightingale starts to sing,
His melodies dance on the breeze like a fling.
But wooing the bugs is quite a chore,
One flies too close, the feast is no more!

With warbles that echo, echo and sway,
He's the comedy star of the woodland play.
As crickets chime in, joining the fun,
The symphony plays until night is done.

The Glyphs of Softly Fallen Leaves

Leaves tumble down like clumsy old friends,
Each twist and turn a laughter lends.
An acorn rolls past, plotting a scheme,
To crown a brave oak, oh what a dream!

With every crunch, the critters all cheer,
For autumn's antics are surely here.
Beneath the great oaks, they hold a dance,
In a swirl of leaves, they prance and prance.

Echoes of Solitude in the Trees

In the woods where whispers play,
A squirrel sings, in a silly way.
Branches sway with a gleeful hum,
While rabbits laugh, saying, "Here we come!"

A raccoon jives with a funky twist,
Chasing fireflies, he can't resist.
Branches bend, with giggles abound,
In the green, joy can always be found.

The forest holds a secret dance,
Where leaves flutter, and critters prance.
With every step, they spin and glide,
Sharing chuckles, side by side.

So listen close to nature's jest,
Where even trees have fun at their best.
In solitude, hear the laughter score,
A concert of whimsy forevermore.

The Lost Verses of the Verdant Realm

In a glade where the wild things roam,
The flowers plot to call this home.
A daisy jokes, with petals spread,
"Oh look, I'm tall!"—but it's all in the head.

A snail with style takes quite the stroll,
Wearing a shell, he's on a roll.
He winks at trees, in suits of green,
Their laughter rings, like a whimsical scene.

The frogs compose a pond-side beat,
Jumping in sync, they can't be beat.
Nature's humor, bold and bright,
Turns every day into pure delight.

These verses lost have now been found,
In the vibrant hues of giggles unbound.
So let the woodland revel in glee,
With tales of mirth from each little tree.

A Tapestry of Nature's Choir

In the tapestry where critters sing,
The birds compete for the title of king.
A chipmunk chirps with flair and pride,
While the fox rolls his eyes and hides.

The leaves rustle in grand delight,
As the sun dips low, painting the night.
With each note, laughter fills the air,
Creating a symphony beyond compare.

A raccoon on stage steals the show,
Wearing a hat made of snow.
The crowd goes wild, a joyous cheer,
Nature's choir, harmonious and clear.

In this world where silly reigns,
Every creature breaks their chains.
Together they dance, twirl, and sway,
A fabric of fun, come what may.

The Air Thrum of Cedar Dreams

In the thrum of air, where laughter floats,
The cedar trees tell the goofiest jokes.
A woodpecker cracks up, pecking away,
While the wind hums a tune of play.

A shadow darts, a mischievous sprite,
Hides behind trunks, ready for the fright.
But laughter erupts from both sides,
Under the canopy where humor resides.

The clouds overhead join in the fun,
Casting funny shapes in the setting sun.
With every chuckle, the world feels bright,
In the embrace of nature, pure delight.

So let the cedars sway and beam,
In the rhythm of life, let's follow the theme.
For every moment in this wooded dome,
Is a serenade inviting us home.

Glistening Tears of Dawn

Morning's giggle wakes the trees,
With sunbeams dancing on the breeze.
A squirrel slips, thinks it's all a game,
While birds are strutting just the same.

Each raindrop forms a tiny hat,
Upon the head of a chubby cat.
It sneezes loud, the leaves all shake,
They laugh together by the lake.

The flowers chuckle, colors bright,
As butterflies take off in flight.
A rabbit winks with cheeky flair,
Stiff-legged dances fill the air.

And in the light, the world is jest,
Nature's laugh, it knows what's best.
With glistening tears that sparkle free,
The dawn unveils its symphony.

Beneath the Veil of Twilight

As daylight dips, the fireflies zoom,
Wearing tiny hats, they light the gloom.
They tangle in the evening's quilt,
Creating giggles without guilt.

A cricket starts its evening show,
With comical tunes that ebb and flow.
The owls are grinning, casting winks,
While underfoot, the shadowed sphinx.

The moonrise dons a wink of cheese,
As frogs gather round with joyful pleas.
They croak in rhythm, tickle the night,
Turning every fear into delight.

Thus twilight wraps the world in cheer,
With whispers soft that all can hear.
Beneath the veil, the laughter flows,
Amidst the flicker of firefly shows.

Whispers from the Canopied Depths

In leafy halls where secrets stir,
The gnomes convene and start to blur.
They swap tall tales of wobbly trees,
While ticklish vines sway in the breeze.

A raccoon peeks from a hollow trunk,
Wearing a vest, all grubby and punk.
He shares his snacks in a sneaky way,
As butterflies beg him for a play.

From canopies, the laughter echoes,
As squirrels flip over like acrobats, their shows.
Mice play charades in the cool dim light,
Creating chaos that feels just right.

So let us wander where giggles reign,
And paint the leaves with joy, not pain.
For in the depths of nature's heart,
The funniest tales will never part.

Chronicles of the Woodland Beyond

In the forest, tales are spun,
Of clumsy deer that prance for fun.
They trip on roots and land in mud,
And giggles bubble like a flood.

Gather round, the owls do tease,
With wise old eyes and plotting schemes.
They've seen it all, the funny quirks,
Of wiggly worms and dancing smirks.

The streams are laughing, splashing bright,
With fish that leap and wiggle right.
While frogs in chorus sing a tune,
As if they're planning a silly moon.

And when at dusk the stories soar,
The woodland echoes, always more.
With Chronicles that tickle the mind,
Joy is hidden everywhere you find.

Elysian Whispers of the Evergreens

In a forest where giggles grow,
Trees wear hats made of snow.
Squirrels debate who's king of the hill,
While mushrooms dance to their own thrill.

Breezes play tricks, tickle leaves,
Trees chuckle, hiding their thieves.
A lost frog croaks an off-key tune,
And owls hoot laughing at the moon.

Beneath a bough, a fox tells tales,
Of shadowy knights and scaly snails.
With whispers of laughter in the air,
Nature's joy is beyond compare.

Amidst the branches, a party awaits,
With acorns popping like tiny plates.
Laughter echoes through the high pine,
In this forest, everybody's divine.

The Timelessness of Nature's Song

Barking trees sing roundelay,
Chirping crickets join the fray.
With every leaf a giggle spins,
As the sun winks, and the fun begins.

A race of ants with a silly plan,
To carry crumbs like a marching band.
They stumble and tumble, oh what a sight,
While the butterflies laugh in delight.

Golden rays turn shadows to jest,
As nature puts levity to the test.
A snail slips on humor, what a funny chase,
In this timeless realm, joy's the pace.

When dusk settles, the stars reveal,
A midnight comedy, oh so surreal.
Laughter twinkles in night's embrace,
In the silence of magic, find your place.

Rhapsody of the Moonlit Forest

Moonbeams ripple, a shimmering dance,
In a wood where the chortles prance.
Owls wear glasses, look quite sage,
While fireflies scribble on nature's page.

A deer prances in polka dots,
Giggles spreading from humor's hot spots.
The brook burbles jokes, oh what a tease,
Nature's laughter echoes through the trees.

Rabbits tell tales of legendary feats,
While hedgehogs nap in cozy retreats.
Mice play charades by the glow of the moon,
In this rhapsody, all the critters croon.

With each rustle, joy goes around,
In this moonlit stage where wonders abound.
Nature's laughter, a tuneful night,
Where silliness reigns under starlit light.

Tones of the Leafy Fortress

In a leafy fortress where quirks reside,
Laughter builds with nature as its guide.
Each leaf a member of the glee club,
Tickling the sun with every scrub.

A hedgehog wearing a tiny crown,
Jokes about the squirrels tumbling down.
Roots join in, spinning tales of yore,
While birds compose tunes from the forest floor.

Laughter bounces off bark and stone,
In this green castle, absurdity's grown.
With acorns rolling into silly games,
Nature's humor has no names.

The trees sway as if in delight,
Whispering tales in the fading light.
In this fortress, fun has its reign,
In the leafy boughs, joy will remain.

When the Pines Begin to Sing

When the pines start to hum a tune,
Squirrels dance, chasing the moon.
The owls chuckle, dressed in style,
Funky tunes that make us smile.

The branches sway like they know how,
A secret party starts right now.
The acorns drop, a bop and roll,
Nature's DJ, in control!

With every breeze, a giggling breeze,
The pinecone crew starts with a tease.
Barking dogs join the crazy spree,
While rabbits hop with wild glee!

So when the pines sing loud and clear,
Grab your friends and bring some cheer!
For in the woods, with trees so grand,
There's laughter waiting, close at hand.

The Crescent Moon's Embrace

In the night, the moon does prance,
A silly orb in a dreamy dance.
Stars giggle, tickled by the light,
As crickets tune their songs just right.

The shadows stretch, then duck and dive,
While fireflies buzz, they come alive.
'Hey, what's that?' the critters say,
In the moon's embrace, they'll surely play.

Bunnies hop, a moonlit race,
Chasing dreams in a starry space.
With every wiggle and every leap,
They laugh and bounce, no time for sleep!

So when the crescent glows above,
Join the jest, and share your love!
For in the night, with joy we sing,
Misfit critters, feeling king!

Ballad of the Whispering Winds

The winds are gossiping, can't you tell?
Whispering secrets, casting a spell.
They tickle leaves with laughter bright,
Dancing shadows under the light.

"Did you hear about the oak tree's hat?"
"Yeah, it's wild, I saw it chat!"
The pine trees giggle at the scene,
As breezes drift through spaces green.

'Round the rocks, they swirl and play,
Messy strands in a grand ballet.
Nature's jesters, oh what a sight,
Silly winds weaving pure delight!

So next time you feel a cheeky breeze,
Remember it's sharing jokes with ease.
The winds are here for a joyful ride,
Turning moments into fun-filled stride!

Traces of Light Beneath the Leaves

Beneath the leaves, a giggle hums,
The sunlight flickers, tickling bums.
With patches bright, the forest grins,
As playful shadows twirl like twins.

A rabbit hops, and then a trip,
Over roots, it starts to flip!
A squirrel laughs, "You should have seen,
The dance you did, it was too keen!"

Amidst the green, where breezes play,
Light dips low in a cheeky way.
The laughter carries, soft and sweet,
In joyful whispers, all repeat.

So when you stroll where light slips through,
Join the fun, embrace the view.
For laughter's trace, beneath the trees,
Will always put your heart at ease.

When the Land Drew Breath

The trees all giggled, roots wiggled in dance,
While squirrels in bow ties took their chance.
Beneath the wide sky, the grass whispered tales,
Of daffodils plotting wobbly trails.

Breezes tickled leaves, a ticklish brigade,
Birch trees chimed in, their voices displayed.
Mushrooms wore hats, on the ground they would prance,
A picnic of fungi, in a whimsical trance.

In the land of the funny, all nonsense feels right,
As owls with glasses debate through the night.
Rabbits in capes hold a silly debate,
On carrot elections—who's destined for fate?

When moonlight chuckles and laughter is near,
The trees hold their breath, not wanting to hear.
Every rustle a joke, every trunk a joke-teller,
In this lively forest, all becomes a jester.

The Voice of the Starlit Canopy

The stars winked down, a playful old crew,
As the wind sings sweet tunes, swirling the dew.
Crickets in tuxedos began to recite,
Verse after verse of their nonsense delight.

Clouds formed a quilt, soft laughter in seams,
While raccoons held court—supreme kings of dreams.
With moonlight as spotlight, they strut on the stage,
Proclaiming that snacks must be served with a wage.

Fireflies flashed rhythm, a glowing parade,
With every flicker, a jester was made.
Dancing through brush like a disco so bright,
The forest is laughing, out under the night.

Whispers of humor float through the trees,
Bumblebees buzzing in comical ease.
Chirps from the branches, a radio play,
A symphony silly, come laugh and we'll stay.

Threads Woven in Nature's Lyric

In the tangle of vines, antics unfold,
A spider spins yarns that are quirky and bold.
Ants don their uniforms, parading their strength,
As jittery jays argue their winged length.

With every small bud, there's a rumor to share,
While daisies in bonnets gossip with flair.
Bouncing sunflower heads join in the jest,
Polishing petals, they preen with their best.

Breezes weave tales, a metaphor plot,
Of hedgehogs in dance shoes—how silly, they trot!
While mushrooms debate their favorite kind of stew,
The creek laughs along, its giggles are true.

Through roots that entwine, the stories are spun,
Amidst the green laughter, together as one.
The tapestry grows, brimming with cheer,
Nature's own humor, forever sincere.

The Reverie Amidst the Trees

Beneath boughs of thought, the mind takes a stroll,
Where chuckles are lifted, like a light-hearted goal.
Trees wear their coats, some frayed at the seams,
As thoughts sprout laughter, like whimsical dreams.

A bear with a bowler sits sipping his tea,
While skunks write a memoir—oh, what could it be?
The pinecones are jesters, their tales poke fun,
At squirrels doing flips, soaking in sun.

With each rustle of leaves, wisecracks take flight,
As gophers in shades squeak out jokes of the night.
The squirrels pass the popcorn, it's movie time fun,
While branches hang low, loading laughter by the ton.

In this forest of giggles, the fables afford,
A stylish display of nature's own word.
Where whimsy and wonder twine hand in hand,
The revelry echoes through this vibrant land.

Enchanted Serenade of the Understory

In the glade, the critters dance,
A squirrel twirls, lost in a trance.
The toad croaks low, with gusto and cheer,
While rabbits giggle, no hint of fear.

Amidst the roots, the secrets lie,
A raccoon juggles beneath the sky.
The laughter echoes, a joyful sound,
Where nature's jesters abound all around.

Beneath the leaves, the shadows play,
A worm sings loud—what a funny display!
The ladybugs clap, the beetles spin,
In this merry world, let the fun begin!

With every rustle, a chuckle takes flight,
The breeze carries whispers, a pure delight.
Nature's symphony, a rib-tickling show,
In the quiet woods, where giggles will grow.

Refrains from the Ancient Cedar

The wise old tree, with its twisted grin,
Branches whisper tales, let the laughter begin!
A chipmunk jokes, with a twinkle so bright,
While owls hoot softly, drifting into the night.

From faraway places, the winds bring news,
Of creatures with antics, oh, the laughs they'll choose!
A fox wearing socks, oh, what a sight,
In this woodland tale, everything's light!

As squirrels debate on who has the best stash,
The hedgehogs chuckle, no need for a clash.
With each bumblebee buzzing a silly old tune,
The forest erupts with a jovial swoon!

So gather around, let's share in the jest,
In the heart of the woods, we all feel blessed.
With humor entwined in every tight knot,
The ancient cedar smiles, oh, what a plot!

The Call of the Whispering Glade

Whispers float through the dappled light,
A porcupine prances, such a comical sight!
The frogs play piano on lily pad keys,
Laughing in harmony, swaying with ease.

An ancient lizard claims he can fly,
While fireflies wink as they flit by.
A parade of critters, with antics galore,
Bringing the giggles, and plenty of more!

Amidst the tall grass, a dance-off ensues,
The ants in a line, with their wiggly moves.
Each twist and turn, a cacophony of fun,
As audience critters cheer, "You've already won!"

With light-hearted joy, the glade comes alive,
In every nook, there's laughter to thrive.
Let the forest rejoice with a merry old tune,
As the moon smiles wide, beneath the stars' swoon.

The Sigh of Distant Pines

In the distance, pines nod, oh so wise,
Telling tall tales beneath sunny skies.
An owl makes puns, with a wink and a grin,
While the playful wind says, "Let's all join in!"

A bear with a hat struts down the lane,
Twirling his cane, like a waltz in the rain.
The bunnies applaud, as they tap their feet,
To the rhythm of fun, life's ultimate treat.

Nearby, a fox tells the best of his jokes,
Beneath the cascade of rustling oaks.
Each chuckle spills out, like bubbles in a stream,
In this whimsical place, everything's a dream!

So gather your friends, and join in the cheer,
As laughter and joy ring out crystal clear.
For in this sweet land of the pines up high,
Lies a world made of giggles—come, give it a try!

Echoing Hearts Beneath the Tree Canopy

Underneath the leafy shade,
Squirrels dance in serenade.
Acorns drop with quite a thud,
It's quite a nutty neighborhood.

Laughter rings in leafy halls,
As jaybirds mimic silly calls.
Rabbits hop in dapper coats,
Stealing snacks from dinky goats.

A family of raccoons plays,
Holding raucous, wild parades.
Nature's fun, a grand affair,
With silly antics everywhere!

Glimmers of joy, a sight to see,
In the shade of the big old tree.
As wise old owls watch from yonder,
The day's a joke, just ponder!

In the Arms of the Gentle Giants

Beneath the giants, tall and proud,
They hold their secrets, soft and loud.
A gopher jokes, a worm too spry,
With laughter reaching way up high.

The trees just chuckle, leaves a-flutter,
As squirrels engage in acorn clutter.
Bumbling bees make quite the fuss,
As crickets nod to their own bus.

Beneath these arms, the stories blend,
Of silly tales that never end.
A cozy nook of nature's cheer,
Where laughter blooms both far and near.

Behold the dance of whimsy here,
The gentle giants hold us dear.
In every trunk, a giggle waits,
Nature's love, in funny states.

Whispers of Old Wounds

In the rustling leaves, whispers spin,
Each wind a chuckle, a cheeky grin.
Old wounds laugh, they dance in time,
In the grand old trees, a silly rhyme.

Mushrooms sprout in places new,
With polka dots of every hue.
They jiggle gently, bringing cheer,
Transforming wounds from doubt to spear.

Caterpillars waltz with glee,
Making a show for all to see.
The cracked old bark tells tales so grand,
Of silly pranks across the land.

As shadows trot and memories hum,
We weave our stories, let's have fun.
With every rustle, laugh along,
In the leaves where we belong!

Tides of Echoing Moments

Moments flow like waves at night,
Bouncing around, oh what a sight!
Each grin a ripple, laughter swells,
With silly secrets that nature tells.

A rabbit's hop, a bird's smooth glide,
In harmony, they glide and slide.
A woodland rave, oh what a show,
As bright moonlight sets hearts aglow.

Each echo, a jest, a burst of fun,
United in laughter, oh what a run!
The murmurs twist like a playful breeze,
In a dance of moments that joyfully tease.

Catch the tides of this merry spree,
Where giggles flow, wild and free.
In the heart of it all, we find delight,
As each moment dances into the night!

Cascading Melodies of Peace

In the woods where squirrels dance,
A tune emerges by chance.
Birds chirp in a jagged line,
Nature's band, oh how divine!

Laughter echoes with the breeze,
Trees shake with playful ease.
A rabbit joins the jolly show,
Tap dancing on his toes, oh so low!

Bees buzz in harmony bright,
Chasing shadows, what a sight!
While frogs croak in goofy time,
A hilarious rhythm, oh so prime!

Underneath the moon's soft glow,
The forest holds its evening show.
Every creature plays along,
In this sweet, cascading song!

Mirage of Cedar-colored Dreams

In a land where trees wear hats,
Dreaming squirrels chat with bats.
A pine-cone falls with goofy grace,
The head of a capricious race!

Wishing rocks begin to roll,
Spreading giggles, heart and soul.
A cedar tree winks its eye,
Who knew trees could be so spry?

Caterpillars crawl in line,
Dancing like they're feeling fine.
In this dream of leafy hues,
Each step's a chance to snooze!

As the sun begins to set,
We laugh—oh, what a silly bet!
In this mirage of charm and cheer,
Life's a circus, never fear!

Footprints in the Silvered Earth

Tiny prints upon the ground,
What pranks have they confound?
A raccoon with a mischievous grin,
Loves the chaos about to begin!

A hedgehog pulls a sneaky stunt,
Rolling past while on a hunt.
Each footprint tells a tale untold,
Of laugh and fun, a sight to behold!

Giggling grasses sway and tease,
As critters join the floral breeze.
In this silvered earth so bright,
Wonders play in plain sight!

With every step, a chuckle rises,
Life's tapestry filled with surprises.
In the footprints' dance, so free,
Joy's the path we all can see!

Songs Carried on the Evening Breeze

The evening hums with silly tunes,
As stars peek through the evening dunes.
A cricket choir sings in jest,
Nature's concert, oh what a fest!

The fireflies join with glowing flair,
Twinkling lights dance in the air.
A raccoon strums a moonlight song,
Making mischief all night long!

The breeze knows every secret laugh,
Tickling trees in a happy half.
Branches sway in sync, so bold,
Whispering tales of joy retold!

As shadows flit and giggles ring,
All creatures leap and dance and sing.
In the night, they find their bliss,
Every note a dreamy kiss!

Beneath the Stars, the Universe Listens

Under twinkling lights so bright,
Frogs croak songs, a funny sight.
Crickets chirp in perfect tune,
While owls gossip 'neath the moon.

Squirrels dance with acorn flair,
Twirling 'round without a care.
Stars above begin to giggle,
As fireflies swirl and wiggle.

Wishes float on puffs of air,
A comet's tail tosses, fair!
Laughter rumbles through the night,
While the universe holds tight.

Each wish whispered makes them grin,
Cacti chuckle, where they spin.
Beneath this vast, celestial dome,
Nature laughs while we call home.

When Mosses Sing of Forgotten Times

Mosses murmur secrets deep,
In forest beds, where critters creep.
Fungi dance a jig so sly,
As lazy ants just wonder why.

A snail's ballet on the stone,
Wears a crown of leaves, alone.
Whispers weave through trees alive,
While beetles buzz and dive.

Every patch of green sings out,
Tales of joy and silly shout.
Nature's choir never stops,
Even when the raindrop plops.

Forgotten times like ribbons flow,
With laughter from the earth below.
In the mossy, twilight glow,
Life's odd tunes begin to grow.

The Reflective Silence of Earth

In silence wrapped, Earth's humor blooms,
Laughter crackles in dusty rooms.
The rocks just chuckle, so they say,
While flowers dance in sweet ballet.

Trees lean in to share a joke,
While rivers giggle, never choke.
The sun winks down with bright delight,
As clouds play hide-and-seek in flight.

Critters pause to catch a breath,
In this charm of life and death.
A giggly breeze sways low and high,
As laughter tickles, floating by.

Reflections dance on quiet streams,
While Earth whispers whimsical dreams.
In every crack and crevice, cheer,
Life's satire sings, ever near.

A Serenade Among the Timbers

Listen close to woodlands cheer,
Rustling leaves, a song sincere.
Chipmunks chatter, squirrels flip,
In this symphony, none can skip.

Stumps recall the tales of yore,
Knots and knots, a fun folklore.
Beetles tap a beet rhythm wide,
As pine trees sway with goofy pride.

Branches creak with total glee,
Echoing laughter from every tree.
Nature's band begins to play,
While raccoons sneak in disarray.

The timbered stage, a joyful play,
As creatures join in the display.
A serenade that skips and hops,
In the heart of woods, laughter pops!

When the Nightingale Sings Softly

In a garden where the daisies sway,
A nightingale sings in a cheeky way,
He teases the flowers, a laugh they make,
As he wiggles around, a humorous shake.

The sun sets low, the crickets join,
With chirps and giggles, they all conjoin,
A squirrel jumps high, falls flat on his back,
Echoing laughter, as night starts to crack.

The moon, a witness to this merry scene,
Casts light on the antics, a radiant sheen,
In the realm of stars, where spirits align,
Even the owls must pause and dine.

A giggle in the breeze makes time stand still,
Winking at the fireflies, joining the thrill,
In the world of characters, so quirky and bright,
The nightingale croons until morning light.

Beneath the Veil of Forest Dreams

In the heart of the woods, where the giggles roar,
A fox in a hat tells tales of folklore,
He trips over roots, with a wink and a grin,
As he dances through shadows, cheeky mischief within.

Beneath the tall trees, where dreams take flight,
A bear wears a bowtie, something's not right,
He juggles some berries, with a clumsy flair,
As laughter goes echoing, a melodious rare.

With each rustling leaf, a joke unfolds,
The whispers of nature, a mystery told,
A party of critters, beneath shimmering beams,
As day turns to night, in this land of dreams.

The brook giggles softly, a bubbly delight,
Reflecting the moon, a whimsical sight,
In this magical place, where the fun never ends,
Each nook holds a secret, with laughter it blends.

Lament of the Lone Traveler

A traveler wanders, with shoes full of holes,
Whistling a tune, while stepping on coals,
He trips on a stone, tumbles down with a shout,
His map now a napkin, oh what's this about?

He meets a wise owl, with spectacles low,
Who offers some wisdom, but forgot where to go,
With feathers all ruffled, they giggle and chime,
Sharing the mishaps of traveling time.

A squirrel with a monocle, takes the lead,
Pointing to berries, that nobody needs,
Left and then right, they both turn around,
Where the laughter of nature is always profound.

At dusk, the lone traveler sits with his crew,
Whoever may join him, they laugh the night through,
For every lost path and each silly blunder,
Turns into stories, a joyous wonder.

The Songbird's Last Serenade

The songbird perches on a branch of delight,
With a croon and a caw beneath the moonlight,
She sings to the frogs, who join in with glee,
While a turtle tap dances, oh look at me!

Her voice floats like petals in a whimsical tune,
A raccoon bumbles in, wearing a spoon,
As crickets applaud, with their chirps in a flare,
The whole forest revels, in this funny affair.

With every last note, a tickle in the air,
She twirls and she spins, without a single care,
A splash of confusion, the stars blink awake,
As laughter ignites, the night starts to shake.

With a wink to the crowd, she bids them farewell,
As the laughter echoes, like stories to tell,
In the calm of the night, where the animals buzz,
The songbird's last serenade lingers because.

The Language of the Resting Wind

In the woods where whispers play,
Squirrels argue, come what may.
Leaves giggle as they wave hello,
While mushrooms plot a dance-so-slow.

The breeze carries tales untold,
Of acorns wearing hats of gold.
Rabbits hop with so much flair,
While crickets hum without a care.

A fox prances with a twiggy crown,
Claiming victory, never a frown.
Nature jests in its own sweet way,
Bringing laughter to the play.

So lean in close and lend an ear,
Join the forest cheer, my dear.
With each gust, let your spirits rise,
For humor in the woods is wise.

Intricacies of Twilight's Lullaby

When day says bye with a sleepy grin,
The night's ball starts to spin.
Owls hoot jokes as they take flight,
While fireflies waltz in the fading light.

Bats in capes, a mischievous bunch,
Delve into shadows, prepare for a lunch.
A pizza slice flies by with a squeak,
What a feast! Oh, so unique!

The sky erupts in colors bright,
As stars giggle, sparkling with delight.
Each twinkling star a silent tease,
Making wishes float on a gentle breeze.

So sway to the songs, both silly and sweet,
In this ridiculous night, take a seat.
The moon grins down, mischievous and bold,
Telling tales that never grow old.

Cadence of the Woodland Faerie

In the grove where laughter grows,
Faeries dance in colorful clothes.
They trade puns like shining coins,
Tickling toadstools, causing joy to join.

Wand in hand, a faerie spins,
With giggles that lead to silly wins.
The trees sway, joining the play,
Leaves laughing in their leafy ballet.

Bumblebees buzzing with delight,
Join the jamboree of the night.
Jellybeans rain down from the sky,
As faerie jokes make the flowers sigh.

So tiptoe gently, feel the cheer,
In this realm where pranks appear.
For every flicker, there's a jest,
In the heart of the faerie fest.

The Forgotten Echoes of Nightfall

As dusk spills paint in a sleepy town,
The owls put on their wise old gown.
Ghosts tell stories, quite absurd,
While shadows dance without a word.

The moonlight finds a comedy stage,
Where echoes giggle, causing a rage.
Cats don top hats, a fancy feast,
As whispers swirl like a joyful beast.

Crickets chirp their nightly score,
While raccoons rummage for a midnight lore.
A dance-off starts with creatures bold,
Each step a tale, both new and old.

So join the fun in the cool night air,
Where echoes play and laughter's rare.
For in the gloom, such whims abound,
And all things funny can be found.

The Enigma of the Hollow Wood

In the hollow wood the squirrels play,
Chasing each other without delay.
But what they see, we cannot know,
Perhaps a dance or a bread dough throw.

The trees all giggle, their leaves a-flutter,
Waiting for tales of the silly nutter.
With acorns acting in a circus show,
While chipmunks snicker, putting on a glow.

Pet frogs croak out a soggy tune,
As owls hoot in squeaks like a balloon.
Raccoons wear masks, just like at prom,
In a wood where the weird feels like home.

So if you wander, don't feel absurd,
Join the funny antics, not a word heard.
In this magical maze, laughter is key,
To dance with the winds, just a little spree.

Lyrical Secrets of the Hollow Grove

In the hollow grove, where giggles grow,
The whispers of winds put on a show.
A fox in socks, with a curious pout,
Plays peek-a-boo till the sunlight's out.

Birds flaunt their colors, like fashion from France,
While rabbits jump into a bright little dance.
The daisies join in, twirling in glee,
Swaying to rhythms, oh so carefree!

Every tall tree has secrets to share,
With bushes conspiring, plotting a dare.
A melody here, a chuckle right there,
In the forest, things happen unaware!

So listen closely, take note of the fun,
In the hollow grove, joy weighs a ton.
Each leaf is a giggle, each breeze is a laugh,
A whimsical world, let's dance on the path.

The Light That Danced on Bark

The light that danced on the rugged bark,
Played tag with shadows until it was dark.
A squirrel named Dave said, "I've got a plan!"
He wore a bow tie—this dapper young man!

Fireflies twinkled, a disco ball bright,
As crickets marched forth, ready to fight.
With bushes in skirts, and vines intertwined,
The party commenced, just nature aligned!

Through giggles and whispers, the night came alive,
A glow-in-the-dark bee started to jive.
"Let's take a selfie, I'm feeling quite bold!"
Said a gathering group, as the moments unfold.

When morning arrives, they'll laugh in the shade,
For now, with each flicker, their memories made.
In the light that giggles on bark, it's clear,
Nature's own party, we all must adhere!

A Harmonious Shade of Life

In the harmonious shade, where the fun is rife,
Grouchy old turtles shake off the strife.
They'll form a band, play tunes that surprise,
While ants tap-dance, oh how they rise!

The daisies chat, all whimsy and bold,
Sharing their stories, sweet and untold.
Caterpillars sashaying on soft, leafy floors,
Dreaming of wings, but for now, they adores.

Bubbles of laughter lift high in the trees,
Mice twirl and whirl, catching soft breezes.
A raccoon with flair struts wearing a crown,
Commanding the stage, never to frown.

Now, under the sun's warm, sunny glance,
The creatures of life engage in a dance.
So join in the fun, feel nature's delight,
In a shade filled with laughter, everything feels right.

Twilights Weaved in Fern

Beneath the leaves, the critters play,
A squirrel danced, then dashed away.
The fireflies flicker, shine so bright,
While frogs croak tunes, oh what a sight!

The moon sneezes, what a sound!
The night, it giggles all around.
With ferns that shimmy, sway and bend,
The woodland's laughter knows no end!

A hedgehog spins in wild delight,
As shadows blend with the twilight.
The breeze enlivens each funny prance,
In nature's odd yet merry dance!

So join the fun beneath the stars,
Where even trees wear silly jars.
In leafy realms where spirits throng,
Life's a jest, a bright, bold song!

The Fable of Waning Light

A tale unfolds as daylight dips,
The sun bids adieu with funny quips.
A raccoon dons a tiny hat,
While owls debate who's chubby or fat!

As dusk drapes smiles upon the ground,
Grasshoppers chirp a wacky sound.
The clouds wear pillows, soft and white,
Such silly shapes in fading light!

With shadows stretching, arms wide and free,
They play hide and seek behind a tree.
A butterfly flits, a giggle spry,
While stars appear with a wink, oh my!

The night unfolds its playful guise,
Where laughter sneaks in every size.
With every chuckle 'neath the moon,
The fable sings a merry tune!

Melodies in the Cedar Mist

In cedar groves where whispers breeze,
The critters clown in perfect freeze.
A mouse in shoes struts with great flair,
While chipmunks mimic—oh, what a pair!

Mist wraps around with a giddy swoop,
As squirrels concoct their nutty loop.
The wind hums tunes of cheerful glee,
While bushes wiggle like they're at sea!

With branches swaying, soft and bright,
Trees join in laughter, oh what a sight!
Each petal bursts into a snicker,
As flowers gossip, getting quicker!

In this delight of nature's hands,
All join the fun across the lands.
So dance with glee, let worries flee,
In this misty, merry jubilee!

Wistful Harmonies of Nature

In twilight's grip, the breezes tease,
Whiskers twitching on the fur of bees.
Crickets jive with their happy feet,
While worms do flips in rhythmic beat!

Amidst the leaves, a grumpy toad,
Is croaking jokes on his lumpy road.
The trees, they chuckle, swaying slow,
As nocturnal critters put on a show!

With whispers caught on starlit breath,
Life plays peek-a-boo with playful death.
A dance-off brews in moonlit beams,
Where laughter springs from wildest dreams!

So entertain the night with cheer,
Where nature's whimsy draws us near.
In every sigh and happy hum,
Funny harmonies will surely come!

The Stillness of the Woodland Breeze

In the woods where squirrels play,
A breeze whispers and twirls all day.
Leaves dance like they're in a ballet,
But I tripped and fell—oh, what a display!

The owls chuckle from their high seat,
As I try to get up on my two feet.
Nature laughs, it's quite the treat,
While the chipmunks watch me, so discreet.

A twig snaps like a joke well told,
Laughter echoes, both warm and cold.
The trees sway gently, brave and bold,
While I ponder why I'm not sold.

Yet here I remain, a woodland clown,
With leafy confetti adorning my gown.
In this joyous place, I wear my crown,
And with each stumble, I laugh, not frown.

Memory of a Distant Firefly

Once in a field where fireflies gleamed,
I chased them wildly, or so it seemed.
Caught one in a jar, how I beamed,
Until it blinked—what a plot, it schemed!

It winked at me, then promptly flew,
Leaving me with a jar and a boo-hoo.
I've learned that bugs aren't for a stew,
Especially ones with a light show to pursue.

Yet memories flicker, bright and bold,
Of laughter shared and tales retold.
The glow of those bugs, if truth be told,
Was the best fun I had, pure gold.

Now when I sit and the night is clear,
I giggle softly, recalling that cheer.
Great fun awaits when friends are near,
Especially when fireflies appear!

Caress of the Moonlit Glade

In the glade where moonbeams play,
I danced like nobody's watching, hey!
With shadows twirling in a silly ballet,
I stepped on a frog—oh dear, not today!

The trees giggled as I leaped around,
The sleepy night critters barely made a sound.
Each slip and slide was quite profound,
With nature's laughter all around.

A raccoon peeked from a bush nearby,
As I attempted a graceful fly.
But tripping over roots made me sigh,
Now I'm the jester, oh me, oh my!

Yet the moon above shines bright and clear,
With beams of laughter, creating cheer.
In this glade, I shed each fear,
Taking my bow to the night so dear.

Timeless Echoes in the Tall Grass

In tall grass where the secrets lie,
I stumbled upon a cricket's reply.
It chirped a tune, oh me, oh my,
Yet each time I dance, it makes me sigh.

The grass swayed gently in disguise,
With whispers laughing, oh what a surprise!
I twirled and rolled beneath bright skies,
As bugs waved goodnight with tiny goodbyes.

I tried to mimic their happy song,
But croaking like a frog felt so wrong.
Yet every trip made me laugh along,
In this grassy dome, I truly belong.

Now as the sun dips low to rest,
I cherish these moments, feeling blessed.
In echoes here, I jest and jest,
For in the tall grass, I'm a funny guest.

A Symphony of the Forest Heart

In the woods, the critters play,
Chasing echoes of the day.
Squirrels dance with acorn hats,
While raccoons sing in evening chats.

Mushrooms gather for a feast,
Tickling bees, they laugh at least.
A fox juggles forest fruits,
While owls boo in feathered boots.

The breeze whispers secret jokes,
As startled deer become the hoax.
A badger rolls in laughing glee,
Saying, 'Join this fun with me!'

The trees clap their hands in cheer,
For every laugh and every leer.
Together they weave a tale so bright,
In the forest's heart, pure delight.

Laments of the Twisting Branches

Twisted limbs that reach and bend,
Complaining about the wind they send.
'Oh, why must we twist and twirl?
It's a tangled, leafless swirl!'

A branch cries out, 'I need a break!
I dream of flat, not this wild shake!'
The saplings giggle in a line,
'Your complaints are quite divine!'

They all sway in a merry dance,
Lost in the rhythm, they take their chance.
'Embrace the swirl,' the tall ones chant,
'For life's a jig and not a slant!'

And so they laugh, the branches tease,
Bending low to feel the breeze.
In this circus of green and wood,
Their laments turn bright and good.

The Stillness of the Green Cathedral

In the stillness, squirrels sneak,
Whispering secrets in silent peaks.
The shadows chuckle, playing games,
While sunbeams giggle with funny names.

Mossy pews where rabbits sit,
Eavesdropping on a talesplit.
An acorn preacher in a tiny hat,
Preaches wisdom to a curious cat.

'In the hush, we find our joy,
Let's be merry, oh my boy!'
The birds in choir pitch their notes,
As frogs croak out their funny quotes.

So gather round, beneath the green,
Where laughter dances, bright and keen.
In this vast cathedral, so grand,
Hilarity reigns in all the land.

Songs from the Rustic Harp

A harp strums softly in the glade,
Where chipmunks prance, unafraid.
Each note a meal, each chord a feast,
As crickets chirp, a lively beast.

Flickering fireflies join the tune,
Dancing 'neath the silver moon.
A raccoon claps with tiny paws,
Praising the strings with joyful 'laws'.

A bear tries to sing along,
But hums instead a clumsy song.
The trees shake limbs with glee and cheer,
While the rustics laugh, "Come join us here!"

With laughter woven into strums,
The forest swells with merry drums.
In every pluck, a story told,
Of fun and friendship, bright and bold.

Infinite Melodies for the Lost

In the forest where squirrels tap,
Melodies dance, but they wear a cap.
Leaves giggle as breezes sigh,
Whispering secrets to the pie in the sky.

Raccoons strum on a twig guitar,
Beneath the moon, they'll sing bizarre.
A rabbit hops in rhythm, so spry,
While owls laugh at the cat nearby.

Frogs croak beats, a ribbit parade,
Every tune is slightly delayed.
The trees sway with a silly grin,
Each note a riddle, where do we begin?

If you wander too far, take care,
For laughter's lost in the breezy air.
Yet in this wild, wacky spree,
Every lost note is a melody free!

The Language of Bark and Breeze

In the woods, where whispers teem,
Bark tells jokes in an emerald dream.
The pines chuckle, leaves converse,
With a wisdom that sounds quite diverse.

Branches mimic the squirrels' prance,
And the shadows pull you for a dance.
With rustling stories loud and clear,
You'll laugh with the critters, have no fear!

The wind carries tales from afar,
About the bird who fancied a star.
Her feathers bright like a comical fringe,
Each flight a story, each twist a binge.

So come to this grove, you silly soul,
Where laughter and whispers form a whole.
In the language of bark and the breeze,
You'll find humor wrapped in the trees!

Whispers of the Twilight Grove

In twilight's glow, the critters meet,
With a chatter that bounces, oh so sweet.
Badgers tell tales of their snack-filled raids,
While fireflies flash out in lively parades.

The old owl hoots, a critic so sly,
As raccoons attempt to dance and fly.
A spin, a twirl, then down they fall,
Laughter echoes through the trees, a call.

Mice gather round, with popcorn in tow,
To watch the antics of nature's show.
"Did you hear," says one, with eyes so wide,
"Last week the crows had a feathered slide!"

So linger a while, let joy ignite,
In whispers and giggles, the forest feels right.
With every laugh, the night grows bright,
In a grove where whimsy takes flight!

Echoes Beneath the Ancient Boughs

Amidst the trunks that stretch and sway,
Echoes of laughter bright up the day.
Squirrels jest with acorns as props,
While chipmunks gather to swap funny flops.

The boughs creak with mirthful delight,
As shadows pinch at the day's last light.
A wise old fox shares his tongue-twisting tale,
Of the time he tried to outrun a snail.

Jokes travel fast on the whispering breeze,
"Why don't trees play hide and seek?" tease.
"Because good luck hiding, they can't help but show,
Their bark's too thick, all the leaves know!"

So dance with the echoes, let laughter abound,
In the hollowed woods where joy's always found.
Under ancient boughs, where giggles blend,
The stories go on, with no need to end!

Murmurs Amongst the Silent Pines

In the forest where squirrels chatter,
A raccoon wears a hat that's too flat.
The trees gossip, their branches sway,
While rabbits dance in their own ballet.

A fox in boots, with style quite bold,
Tells stories of fish caught in the cold.
The owls chuckle, their wisdom so slick,
As the world turns round, they yarn and tick.

A shy deer snorts, a mischievous tease,
It plays pranks on the buzzing bees.
In laughter, the leaves rustle, take flight,
Creating twirls, in the fading light.

The woodland whispers, a curious tune,
As echoing giggles blend with the moon.
Underneath twinkling stars, they'll prance,
In a night where everyone loves to dance.

Veils of Dusk in the Woodland

As day folds into a soft-spoken night,
A hedgehog dons glasses, oh what a sight!
The moon winks down with an impish glow,
While fireflies whisper, 'Come on, let's go!'

A bear steals honey, with a grin so wide,
While raccoons plot their next wild ride.
The trees burst out with giggles so spry,
At the antics of creatures so sly.

An owl hoots jokes, all wise and profound,
While badgers dig deep, looking for sound.
The wind carries laughter, a playful breeze,
Leaving behind chuckles, and soft, swaying trees.

With each gentle shift of the dusk-tinted sky,
Creatures unite in a jubilant sigh.
In this merry realm where the strange is delight,
We dance with our shadows, till morning is bright.

Serenade of the Hidden Glade

In a glade where the mischief unfolds,
A lizard in shades, oh what a bold!
Chasing butterflies, laughing aloud,
With a chirp from the crickets, they gather a crowd.

A playful raccoon with candy striped socks,
Hosts a fiesta amidst glittering rocks.
The vines sway to rhythm, all twirling round,
As melodies bubble from the leaves on the ground.

Beneath the green canopy, giggles arise,
While a bear juggles berries—oh, what a surprise!
The breeze carries stories of laughter and cheer,
As critters convene, year after year.

So dance, little creatures, in moonlight's embrace,
With a wink and a wiggle, join in the race.
In the hidden glade, where the fun never wanes,
The magic of giggles forever remains.

Notes from the Enchanted Canopy

High above, in the branches of green,
A parrot croons softly, a marvelous scene.
With a toucan tapping a funny beat,
They gather together for a whimsical treat.

The branches chuckle, as squirrels debate,
Who can leap higher? Who seals their fate?
With a swing and a twirl, they glide with flair,
In a joyous dance, spun through the air.

A wise old owl tries to join in the fun,
But stumbles and trips, under the moon's run.
The branches all tremble, they shake in delight,
Whispering giggles into the night.

In the enchanted canopy, where laughter reserves,
The heart of the forest beats in swerves.
So merrily they frolic, 'neath the smiling sky,
In this sacred space where the joy is high.

www.ingramcontent.com/pod-product-compliance
Lightning Source LLC
Chambersburg PA
CBHW071836160426
43209CB00003B/320